WE
DECLARE

31 Days of
Intercession
for America

David Kubal

PRAYERSHOP
PUBLISHING
Terre Haute, Indiana

PRAYERSHOP
PUBLISHING

PrayerShop Publishing is the publishing arm of the Church Prayer Leaders Network. The Church Prayer Leaders Network exists to equip and inspire local churches and prayer leaders in their desire to disciple people in prayer and to become a "house of prayer for all nations." Its online store, prayershop.org, offers more than 150 prayer resources for purchase or download.

ISBN (Print): 978-1-970176-35-3
ISBN (E-Book): 978-1-970176-36-0

Printed in the United States of America

CONTENTS

Introduction

". . . Life, Liberty and the pursuit of Happiness."

Those words ring joyfully in our ears because they are fundamental principles embraced in one of the great documents of history: the American *Declaration of Independence.* So invaluable were these inalienable rights to our Founding Fathers that they pledged their lives, fortunes, and sacred honor as they launched a new nation in defense of those rights. More than that, they declared together *"a firm reliance on the Protection of Divine Providence."*

Today, however, many Americans have largely forgotten what those words mean. The gift of life is treated flippantly or worse. Our liberties—especially religious freedom—are goods taken for granted, or perhaps even viewed as societal ills. And the pursuit of happiness is confused with a shallow search for the next high—a chasing after the wind.

I believe you're beginning this *We Declare: 31 Days of Intercession for America* prayer guide because you know that America is in dire need of saving—and you sense that God wants *you* to be part of the rescue plan. I encourage you to take your time reflecting and praying as you read through the daily entries in this guide. Please voice boldly the declarations the Lord places on your heart. We need your heart and your voice!

And know that we at IFA stand ready to help you on this journey. Please don't hesitate to contact me or our staff team at any point, through IFAPray.org or by calling 1-800-USA-PRAY. *We're in this together,* and we'll be declaring light, hope, and wisdom for you as you declare life, liberty, and the pursuit of happiness in your own way over this beautiful land.

May God reinvigorate our nation and truly bless America. Amen.

—Dave Kubal, President and CEO,
Intercessors for America

Declaration 1

Life

The very first gift God gave us is life. Human history begins with the Lord forming Adam's body and breathing life into it. Then, at the focal point of history—the cross of Christ—God makes a way for our spirits and our bodies to live again. Our nation's Founders were right to recognize the fundamental truth that God cherishes human life, that it is an inalienable right which earthly authorities are entrusted with respecting and defending. We believe that God will secure and bless our land as we revitalize a culture that honors the sanctity of human life.

Day 1: Embracing Life

"And this is eternal life, that they know you, the only
true God, and Jesus Christ whom you have sent."
(John 17:3)

As we embark together on this 31-day journey of intercession for America, there is no more fitting a place to begin than here, with a declaration of *life* for the people of our land. Think about it: Every one of our individual stories—not to mention our collective story as the human race—starts with God forming and breathing life into us. He gave us bodies and spirits. And He designed us to live with Him eternally.

Every one of us lost hold of that gift. We all—from Adam to the hundreds of thousands of new lives being born on the very day you are reading this—*we all* have gone astray. We all are stained by sin. We all make choices that set us on a road to physical and spiritual death.

But God. God didn't give up on us. He so cherished us—the lives He breathed into existence—that He devised a radical plan to save us. At the cost of His own life, Jesus atoned for our wrongs. And then He rose. He rose from and defeated death and made a way for us to live again!

That is good news, friends! It's a message of love. It's a message of hope. And it's a word that the people of our land desperately need to hear and to embrace.

It's no secret that we as individuals and as a nation have made choices that are sending us down a dangerous path. If you are beginning this work of intercession, then this reality is probably already heavy on your heart. But remember: Death does not have the last word. Jesus conquered death. He is the way, the truth, and the *life*. That is a victory worth declaring!

PRAY

- ☐ Praise God that He breathed life into us, and He made a way for us to escape the wages of sin and to live again!
- ☐ Pray for the first friend or neighbor who comes to mind. And pray for the next stranger who crosses your path. Pray that somehow today God would break into their day, and that they would see that He loves them and wants them to truly flourish—to be filled with life.
- ☐ Christ is risen! Declare the victory of life over death. Pray that eyes in our nation would be opened and that more hearts will embrace the love, hope, peace, and joy of that reality. Pray that our leaders would help our society to choose a path of life.

ENGAGE

Mail a card to a local government, business, or community leader. Keep it simple. Tell that individual about God's love and gift of life. Invite that person to church. Will the leader respond? You never know until you take a step.

Day 2: Wonderfully Made

*For you formed my inward parts; you knitted me
together in my mother's womb. I praise you, for
I am fearfully and wonderfully made. Wonderful
are your works; my soul knows it very well.*
(Psalm 139:13–14)

When was the last time you looked into a mirror and said to yourself: "I am wonderfully made"? Is there a mirror nearby? How about a camera app on your mobile device? Stop just a minute and try it out.

OK, now look around you; is there someone next to you on a plane or train? Is there a person walking down the street or sitting in a coffeeshop window? Whoever you see, think to yourself: *"That person is wonderfully made."*

This isn't an exercise in vanity or superficiality. No matter who is near you, or what you saw in your reflection, at the core what you saw is beautiful. In Psalm 139 King David reminds us that we are "knitted" by God and that we are "fearfully and wonderfully made." Looking back further, the very first chapter of the Bible tells us that God created man in His own image. Actually, in case we missed the importance of that statement, the Genesis account immediately repeats it by declaring again: *So God created man in his own image, in the image of God he created him; male and female he created them* (Gen. 1:27).

The image of God—what does that mean? That's worth its own 31-day study, but basically, it means that every single person ever "knitted" by God is uniquely and intrinsically special. Our lives are of inestimable worth, not because of anything we have done, but because of Who our Creator is.

Our nation's Founding Fathers understood the fundamental importance of honoring life. That is why it's the first inalienable right listed in the Declaration of Independence. Life is a precious gift from our Creator that human authorities are intended to preserve and protect.

Tomorrow we will turn to interceding in the face of our land's most egregious offense against this basic underpinning of our society. But today, let us celebrate the beauty of every person as being wonderfully made. And let's pray against any action or message in public policy, the media, pop culture, business, or anywhere else that defaces or demeans the sanctity of human life.

PRAY

☐ What was the last advertisement you saw? Did it honor human dignity? Praise God if it did, and pray for change if it didn't.

☐ Take a look at the pop music charts, at the movies, at television, and at video games. Pray for light in all those spaces. Pray for culture influencers to honor human life and not to treat it cheaply or abusively.

☐ Pray specifically against the perpetrators of human trafficking and other forms of modern-day slavery in our nation and around the world. Pray for the release and healing of the victims. May their spirits embrace the truth that they are not property, but people—individuals made in the image of God and loved by Him.

ENGAGE

What songs and videos are most popular in your media market right now? Do they honor the sanctity of the image of God? Perhaps you could post "reviews" on your favorite social media platform. Specify those things in a given song or video that do or do not honor human life, and boldly note why media producers must respect the dignity of human life in their creative works.

Day 3: Defend Prenatal Life

Speak up for those who cannot speak for themselves. (Proverbs 31:8a, NIV).

Did you know that in 2020, Americans welcomed the births of more than 3.6 million babies? Praise God! But in that same year, the pro-abortion Guttmacher Institute calculates, more than 900,000 prenatal lives were terminated. That means roughly one out of every five babies was aborted. Twenty percent of those who were to be in the graduating class of 2038—gone! When was the last time we grieved together over the loss of so many neighbors and loved ones whom we will never know, individuals who were not given the chance to live?

Actually, it is even worse: While we should remember that truly complicated and lose-lose life-threatening situations do occur in some pregnancies, far too many abortions are the result of an abortion-on-demand culture that preys on fear. It's not that individuals were not *given* the chance to live. It's that their lives were *taken*.

If we embrace human life as a gift and an inalienable right—a human right—given to us by God, then abortion-on-demand is one of America's most egregious human-rights abuses. It is a scourge that has destroyed tens of millions of prenatal lives since the infamous Roe v. Wade Supreme Court ruling of 1973, and it continues to corrupt hearts, minds, and the very underpinnings of our land.

Of course, we rejoice that Roe has at last been overturned. But this battle for life is far from over. Just listen to how the news media flood the airwaves and the internet. More and more, abortion is embraced by "progressive" activists and their political allies as something to celebrate, something fundamentally good. And prenatal children and vulnerable women are paying the price.

Not only that, but also the abortion conflict has in effect now shifted from the federal to the state level. Lawmakers in many states have set out to alter their state constitutions to enshrine a so-called "right" to abortion. In a sense, we now face the possibility of 50 Roe v. Wade wars instead of just one.

We must continue to intercede for our land in the face of this horror. Abortion is far more than a political issue. It is a deadly serious crisis in our communities. But this is not a hopeless battle — far from it. Almighty God cares about human life. He created it. He will bring victory as we work to advance a culture that honors the sanctity of human life.

PRAY

☐ Pray for a generation: Roe v. Wade seemed like an unassailable stronghold for abortion in our land. Let us never forget to thank God for the overturn of that tragic ruling. And let us double down on our prayers, refocusing our intercession for God's victory on the state level.

☐ Pray for those government and other community leaders who boldly stand up for the sanctity of life. Ask for clear and winsome messages that sway hearts and minds as they try to speak up for those who cannot speak for themselves.

☐ Pray for a covering of protection over pro-life pregnancy-care centers, in the face of threats from abortion activists. May the members of our communities understand the help and services that such centers are attempting to provide for vulnerable mothers and children.

ENGAGE

Phone a pro-life pregnancy-care center in your community and tell them you appreciate their work advancing a culture of life by serving women and prenatal children who are in need. Ask how you can help.

DECLARATION 2

Religious Freedom

Religious freedom is America's first freedom. Beginning with the Pilgrims, ensuring that America be a place where faith can be lived out freely in daily life has been a core principle for this land. Our nation's Founders affirmed the inalienable right of liberty in the Declaration of Independence, and it is no accident that religious liberty is the very first right upheld in the Bill of Rights. For generations, the United States has been a beacon of light drawing in individuals seeking the freedom to live out their deepest beliefs without fear. But the road has not always been easy, and this remains true today. Let us declare over our nation a return to religious liberty. May we be a land where hearts turn freely to the Lord.

DAY 4: OUR FIRST FREEDOM

And he entered the synagogue and for three
months spoke boldly, reasoning and persuading
them about the kingdom of God. (Acts 19:8)

When you consider the inalienable rights identified in the Declaration of Independence—gifts given to us by God—you see that "liberty" comes right after "life." To truly understand what that liberty is and why it must again be declared and defended in our nation, we need to start with a very specific liberty—religious liberty. Why? Because it is truly our first freedom.

Do you recall the story of the Pilgrims? They hold a special place in our hearts as models for setting aside time to give thanks to God our provider and sustainer. But they also influenced the founding spirit of our nascent nation with their commitment to liberty. The Pilgrims famously arrived in Plymouth, Massachusetts, in 1620 after fleeing persecution for their faith in Europe. Once on this side of the Atlantic, they proceeded to establish the Mayflower Compact— a covenant made expressly before God, and which upheld religious toleration.

Intercessors for America was actually incorporated in Plymouth, so our own organizational development has a spiritual tie to the legacy of the Pilgrims. But the Pilgrim influence extends far beyond IFA, of course. Wave after wave of settlers came here and embraced the Pilgrims' desire to freely pursue faith and freedom, and this became a core element of America's DNA. In fact, religious liberty became so foundational to the framework of our nation that it was actually incorporated as the very first freedom designated for protection in the Bill of Rights.

Now, our nation's Founders didn't come up with this idea on their own. It is based on ideals from the Bible. We know all people have dignity as individuals made in the image of God, and we quickly see in the early chapters of Genesis that part of that dignity includes a freedom to choose right from wrong. In the New Testament, too, we find that Jesus does not force decisions on His hearers and that gospel missions are based on persuasion, not coercion. Ultimately, robust faith requires every one of us to choose for ourselves whom we will serve.

We must focus our intercessory attention on this first freedom—to freely pursue God's heart—for without it we are lost as a nation. May Americans never falter in cherishing the freedom to choose Christ and to worship Him freely. May we be a people of true and robust faith.

PRAY

- ☐ Let's thank God together for the spiritual seeds of thanksgiving, faith, and freedom that the Pilgrims sowed in our land.
- ☐ Pray that America would remain a beacon of light for religious liberty in our world.
- ☐ Gather with another Christian or with a group of intercessors and pray together that Americans would cherish the liberty we have to seek and honor God without government oppression. May our people turn fully to Jesus and freely choose to serve Him wholeheartedly.

ENGAGE

When was the last time you heard a message about religious freedom from the pulpit at your church? Ask your pastor to explore this topic and to speak on the spiritual importance of our first freedom.

Day 5: Religious Freedom Restoration

*Therefore, we are ambassadors for Christ, God
making his appeal through us. We implore you on
behalf of Christ, be reconciled to God.
(2 Corinthians 5:20)*

On a sunny November day in the White House Rose Garden, the president of the United States remarked:

"The free exercise of religion has been called the first freedom, that which originally sparked the development of the full range of the Bill of Rights.

"Our Founders cared a lot about religion. … They knew that religion helps to give our people the character without which a democracy cannot survive. They knew that there needed to be a space of freedom between government and people of faith that otherwise government might usurp."

Those observations came from President Bill Clinton more than 30 years ago at the signing of the Religious Freedom Restoration Act (RFRA). The law many celebrated that day in Washington would require a "compelling government interest" achieved by the "least restrictive means" before the state could override any person's religious objection to a mandate. It was a response to the government's overreaching its authority, and thankfully, one that spurred a bipartisan coalition into action to protect our first liberty.

This might surprise you. In fact, it might seem hard to believe, looking through the lens of today. That's because the RFRA and the principles it represents have fallen out of favor with many.

Those who have embraced the "progressive" left are now angry that the RFRA's common-sense balancing test has achieved its purpose—the shielding of Americans of faith from coercive government mandates. Whether their crusade be the forcing of abortion promotion upon pro-life believers, the requiring of faith-based adoption agencies to recognize same-sex marriage, or any other heavy-handed demand, these progressives are now actively seeking to undermine the RFRA in the minds of Americans in furtherance of their own nefarious ends.

We need a restoration in the hearts and minds of Americans of just how important religious freedom is. The future of our republic depends on laws like the RFRA and the spirit behind them. Now is the time to intercede for our land and our government leaders. We stray from our robust heritage of religious liberty at our own peril.

PRAY

☐ Let us thank God that Americans of different perspectives rallied to the cause of religious freedom in years past, and let us pray that past supporters of the RFRA and related efforts would return to a robust understanding of liberty.

☐ Have you seen someone inappropriately shunned or even disciplined in a school or workplace for carrying a Bible or saying a prayer in public? Pray for that person's strength and courage, and for a remedy that rightly honors their inalienable freedom.

☐ Join with a group of believers in your state to pray specifically that your members of Congress will understand the RFRA and defend its integrity as a law.

ENGAGE

Send a brief handwritten note or electronic message to your congressional representative. Remind him or her that the RFRA is a common-sense balancing test with a successful history and that it must be defended against shortsighted efforts to undermine it.

DAY 6: DEFENDERS OF RELIGIOUS LIBERTY

First of all, then, I urge that supplications, prayers,
intercessions, and thanksgivings be made for all
people, for kings and all who are in high positions,
that we may lead a peaceful and quiet life, godly
and dignified in every way. (1 Timothy 2:1–2)

Why are we spending three days on religious liberty? Because it's *that* important to the survival and flourishing of America. Our Founders knew this, and so must we.

Today, let's intercede specifically for those in positions of authority in our land. Just as they are responsible for honoring God's gift of life, so are they duty-bound to defend every person's God-given right to liberty—especially the freedom to worship and walk in the ways of the Lord.

What does this mean in practice? Well, let's take a look at some recent examples of government leaders getting it right.

The first is a correction of a blatant wrong. Joe Kennedy, a high school football coach, tried to honor Jesus with quiet prayers of gratitude at the 50-yard line after football games. But authorities at his local school district didn't like that, so they terminated his job. Thankfully, though—after years of litigation—the U.S. Supreme Court came down against this discrimination and paved the way for the coach to take to the field once again.

Writing for the court, Justice Neil Gorsuch observed: *"Respect for religious expressions is indispensable to life in a free and diverse Republic."*

Thankfully, we have been able to celebrate a string of court victories for people of faith like coach Kennedy in recent years. A postal worker punished for honoring the Sabbath; an Atlanta fire chief fired for his belief in marriage; faith-based foster providers squashed by authorities in Philadelphia; a pregnancy-care-center group that California demanded promote abortion; a web designer and cakemaker who didn't want to use her artistic gifts to promote same-sex unions — these and more found redress in the halls of justice.

And we see here that government leaders can do right just by respecting faith. But they can also be proactive. They can prioritize religious freedom in their day-to-day work.

One good example of this is found in an executive order President Donald Trump issued in 2020 that focused on the international arena. That directive made clear that religious freedom is a foreign-policy priority—one our nation would "vigorously promote." And this wasn't just words: The order took the important step of putting real money where our nation's mouth is, through foreign aid and diplomacy efforts.

Leaders who will *protect* and *vigorously promote* our first freedom—we need these leaders today.

PRAY

- ☐ Pray over the opening words of the First Amendment in the Bill of Rights: *"Congress shall make no law respecting an establishment of religion, or prohibiting the free exercise thereof."* Pray that everyone serving in the legislative, executive, and judicial branches of government will honor those words.
- ☐ Seek to find out which lawmakers in your community and in our nation go beyond paying mere lip service to religious liberty by putting the money they oversee where their mouth is. Ask God to bless and empower those lawmakers and to raise up many others just like them.
- ☐ Let's thank God for so many victories for faith and freedom in recent years, and let's pray specifically for the justices of the U.S. Supreme Court, that they would continue to make rulings like

the one in coach Kennedy's case. Also let us request that someday they might run out of such cases on the court docket because government leaders have become so good about honoring liberty!

ENGAGE

Call your town, city, or county representative and ask them how they will actively promote respect for religious freedom in your community.

Constitutional Freedom

God always planned for us to be free creatures. He desires that, and we are, by design, at our best when we live lives of liberty on His path of life. As Americans, we often take our freedoms for granted, but our nation's Founders knew the value of those freedoms, and they were right to put strong safeguards around specific liberties. We have already explored our first freedom that is protected in the Bill of Rights, but there are others. Many are currently under attack, as is the system that upholds them, and they need particular attention from people of prayer at this critical time for our nation.

Day 7: Freedom of Speech

*Rather, speaking the truth in love, we are to
grow up in every way into him who is the head,
into Christ. (Ephesians 4:15)*

In the Bill of Rights, just after the guarantee of religious liberty, we find a mandate prohibiting the government from "abridging the freedom of speech." The word "abridging" presupposes the existence of this right. Governments don't grant it—it is one of our inalienable freedoms.

Of course, there are honest debates about the limitations on this right: We can't create a life-threatening situation by falsely yelling *"Fire!"* in a public place, and surely, there should be limits on obscenity and prohibitions on fraud. But many times, the boundary lines we think of regarding speech focus on *what the government can and cannot censor*—what it can *restrict*.

But how about what speech the government can *compel*? If that sounds like it should be a worry only in an obviously authoritarian regime like China or Iran, and not in our own country—well, think again. In this day, we need people of prayer to rally against *coerced* speech.

Let's imagine for a minute: What would you do if the authorities in your state didn't simply make abortion legal, or even merely fund it with your tax dollars, but actually said that you—*you personally*—had to *promote* abortion?

Or, what if the authorities in your state, not content with merely "recognizing" same-sex unions as "marriage," demanded that you—*you personally*—use your words and your creativity to support a redefinition of marriage, sexuality, or gender that you knew was not biblical?

Unfortunately, those are not just "what ifs." State governments have already tried to do both. For example, California passed a law requiring pro-life pregnancy-care centers to advertise for abortion providers. And Colorado has been an infamous battleground for the attempted coercion of both a Christian cakemaker and a Christian graphic artist.

Thankfully, the battles in both those states ended with victories for liberty in the U.S. Supreme Court. In the most recently decided case—*303 Creative v. Elenis,* featuring Lorie Smith—the court explained that having to choose between speaking as the state demands or face heavy sanctions is "more than enough … to represent an impermissible abridgment of the First Amendment's right to speak freely."

But despite how much that may seem like common sense to you or me, this is *not* clear to many Americans. In fact, many of the advocates of those offensive laws are unrepentant. They are blinded by ideologies and agendas that leave no room for dissent.

If we want a land that continues to honor our duty as Christians to speak the truth in love, we need to pray for a recommitment to the freedom of speech.

PRAY

- ☐ Let's thank God for victories in the U.S. Supreme Court for free speech.
- ☐ Pray for local, state, and federal officials to be wary of any rule or regulation that unjustly restricts or coerces speech.
- ☐ Pray for leaders in your church to use their voices to speak the truth in love. After all, if the freedom of speech is not exercised, it can slip away.

ENGAGE

Find a group of prayer warriors in your community and intercede together vigorously for a recommitment to the freedom of speech where you live. Not sure where to find such a group? Let us help!

Day 8: Freedom of the Press

*"Talk no more so very proudly, let not arrogance
come from your mouth; for the Lord is a God of
knowledge, and by him actions are weighed."*
(1 Samuel 2:3)

Do you love the media? I'm guessing you're shaking your head *"no."*

Well, you're not alone. Research released in 2022 by polling company Gallup showed that only 16 percent of U.S. adults say they had "a great deal" or "quite a lot" of confidence in newspapers. For TV, the results were even worse: 11 percent. In fact, more than half of survey respondents said they had *little or no confidence* in TV news (while almost half said the same for newspapers).

Those aren't strong favorability numbers. But then again, you might read them and not really feel shocked. After all, how often have major outlets told only one side of a story about Israel? Or how often have they sidelined or unflatteringly covered pro-life ("anti-abortion") voices while seeming to repeat Planned Parenthood's talking points? Or name your issue.

You don't need to look far in print or online platforms to see that many reporters have personal opinions they're eager to share. It can be difficult to discern where the fact-based reporting ends and the editorializing begins.

The unreliability that mars today's news media is one reason why IFA was launched, and it also regularly populates our Headline Prayer feed. In addition to searching out helpful articles from around the web, we have a team of writers creating original content about timely matters that need to be understood and covered in prayer.

But we also have a heart for the media itself. After all, right after the freedoms of religion and speech in the Bill of Rights is a prohibition on abridging the freedom of the press. Why? Well, our Founders knew that a healthy republic relies on a strong and independent press to keep a scrutinizing eye on government officials—no matter their politics or how upstanding they may seem.

The Virginia Declaration of Rights, an inspiration for the *Declaration of Independence,* said "freedom of the press is one of the great bulwarks of liberty, and can never be restrained but by despotic governments." If we want a truly flourishing land of liberty, we need a free and healthy press. That means we need to ensure the government keeps its hands off the media *and* we must demand that the press stop undermining itself with hubris and irresponsibility.

Let's pause today not simply to disregard the media in disgust, but to actively pray for its rejuvenation as an agent of truth and trust.

PRAY

- ☐ There are many good journalists who want to serve their communities well. Let's pray for those in that important profession who are committed to humbly and confidently restoring trust in their news outlets.
- ☐ Pray for the bias of major media outlets to be exposed and abandoned.
- ☐ Pray that Americans would be able to discern facts from opinions in news shows and publications. And may we all openly yearn for a healthy, robust, trustworthy, and free press.

ENGAGE

Look for one reporter who regularly puts facts above opinion as he or she writes for your local newspaper or serves at your local news station. Send that reporter a note and express your thanks for how he or she is cherishing principles of a free and healthy press. Send a note, too, to that reporter's superiors and recommend he or she be publicly honored and rewarded.

Day 9: Distortion of Justice

Unequal weights are an abomination to the Lord,
and false scales are not good. (Proverbs 20:23)

The next time you visit Washington, D.C., examine the artwork in and around our nation's halls of power. There are stories to be told in those sculptures, reliefs, engravings, and paintings about the values our nation is built on—fundamental beliefs that we are urged not to forget.

In front of the U.S. Supreme Court, for example, you will see at the base of a lamppost a relief of a blindfolded woman holding a sword and scales. This is a depiction of ideal Justice—its power, balance, and impartiality. It is a noteworthy symbol to remind those in or entering the court (and those across the street in the U.S. Capitol) of just how important the embrace of true justice is for our land.

Sadly, the integrity of our nation's justice systems has been compromised. We have talked about fair rulings from the U.S. Supreme Court, but the same cannot be said in the executive branch. While the sword remains sharp, the blindfold appears to have come off, and the scales are using uneven weights.

Think back to the IRS targeting of conservative nonprofit organizations during the Obama administration. Or consider law enforcement's focus on the welfare of abortion clinics versus attention to pro-life pregnancy-resource centers that have been viciously targeted in the wake of Roe v. Wade's overturn. Think, too, of how "progressive" demonstrations are treated versus the rallies of those on the right. And look at investigations into President Trump and his colleagues versus those scrutinizing questionable characters in the orbit of the Clinton and Biden teams.

There is not an equally weighted standard.

The harm in each of these cases is not limited only to the immediate parties. The larger danger is the general erosion of trust in our government, the undermining of our republic that is set up to protect fundamental liberties and ensure our security as a nation.

As we pray today for the integrity of justice to be restored in our land, let's remember the words engraved in another corner of Washington, on the walls of the Jefferson Memorial. There we find this line from the *Declaration of Independence*: "We hold these truths to be self-evident, that all men are created equal, that they are endowed by their Creator with certain unalienable Rights, that among these are Life, Liberty, and the pursuit of Happiness. That to secure these rights, Governments are instituted among Men. … "

May our nation's halls of power treat the people of this land with the equality and respect for liberty we all are due.

PRAY

- ☐ Pray that those entrusted with the powers of our justice system would serve without prejudice or political agenda. May those who would weaponize law enforcement be thwarted.
- ☐ Thank God for public servants who work to the utmost of their ability, but not to favor anyone based on race, religion, wealth, ideology, or any other factor, as they seek a just society.
- ☐ May the people of this nation remember that we are all created equal by God and deserve equal dignity within our justice systems.

ENGAGE

Contact candidates for a local judge or state attorney general post, and ask them how they will actively use the powers of the justice system without impartiality. How will they prevent distortion of justice?

DECLARATION 4

Voting and Elections

Amerivas Founding Fathers believed that God endowed us with inalienable rights to life, liberty, and the pursuit of happiness. We've prayed through the first two of those, but what about that last one? What *is* "the pursuit of happiness"? The Founders weren't concerned with any temporary state of mind. They wanted a nation that ensured an environment conducive to the flourishing that God desired when He created us. As we explore this more fully in the sections ahead, let's turn first to a fundamental system the Founders conceived to undergird *flourishing*. As we pursue the happiness of our land, we must cherish the right to vote, and we must guard the integrity of our elections, because these are part of the fabric of our republic.

DAY 10: IF YOU CAN KEEP IT

*When the righteous are in authority, the people
rejoice; but when a wicked man rules, the people
groan. (Proverbs 29:2)*

In 1787 an inquirer asked Benjamin Franklin what sort of a government the young nation of the United States was to have. Franklin replied: "A republic, if you can keep it."

Franklin was part of the Constitutional Convention that had for months wrestled over what form of constitution our country was to devise, and what priorities it was to embrace. This wasn't an easy process, and Franklin knew that the end result of all the heated debates and exhausting deliberations would not be perfect. However, he and the other Framers also saw that the emerging constitution was a solid framework. It would unite the nation based on God-honoring ideals balanced with guardrails that accounted for the fallenness of human nature. The new document would also allow for measured flexibility by means of amendments, should the need arise.

Now, Franklin and the others believed the framework was important—that's why they poured so much of their energy into it. But they also knew, as Franklin had said, that the citizens of the nascent republic would ultimately be responsible for its success or failure. If the new order was to survive in a dangerous world that was largely hostile to this American experiment, it would require the active involvement of citizens who cherished justice and righteousness. To protect itself from being overrun or suffering self-destruction, the republic would need individuals to spur it on toward its mission of protecting life, liberty, and the pursuit of happiness.

How are we meeting that challenge today? Well, the evidence—the toxicity, violence, and glorification of vices in our society—seems to suggest that we've lost our way. Our republic is teetering on a cliff of destruction. Many have strayed from *the Way,* the Truth, and the Life. They have forgotten the biblical values that are the fabric for any healthy nation.

But that's not all. Christians—active believers—have also lost their way in the public square. Some of us have co-opted our beliefs to "play the game" like the world. Many of us just avoid the messy political arena altogether.

If we want to keep our republic, Christians will need to reengage as salt and light in our communities and halls of power. We need to exhort our neighbors and our nation onward in the *true* pursuit of happiness—the true *flourishing*—with disarming love and the utterance of prophetic truth. Let us pray for the rejuvenation today of a citizenry that can keep our republic strong and secure in the hands of the Lord.

PRAY

☐ When you think of America's virtues, what is the first one to come to mind? Pray for that virtue close to your heart to be reinforced in our culture today.

☐ What about Americas worst sin or vice? What does your spirit specifically grieve over in our society? Pray today for God to do a mighty work to help us all as a nation overcome that darkness.

☐ Pray for Christians in your community to truly be salt and light to their neighbors. Pray for disarming love and prophetic truth to open the door to spiritual healing and new life for our nation.

ENGAGE

Think now about how you can join with a group of prayer warriors on the National Day of Prayer or a similar opportunity in order to intercede together for the people of our land—that we may keep our republic strong.

Day 11: Vote

"Choose wise, understanding, and knowledgeable men from among your tribes, and I will make them heads over you." (Deuteronomy 1:13)

Maybe it's the last item on a busy day's checklist, and it just never gets around to happening. Or perhaps it has rained all day and the prospect of getting out seems unappealing. Or maybe the choices on the ballot are uninspiring.

For whatever reason, during every election, many Americans just don't bother showing up to vote. Even in a banner presidential year like 2020, only about 6 out of every 10 voting-age adults actually head out to the polls, and the numbers are worse during midterms and for state and local races. Many people—including millions of Christians—just decide that voting isn't worth the bother.

This must be unfathomable to people around the world who know what it's like to have no voice in their nation. Certainly, it would have shocked those in previous generations who valiantly fought, bled, and even died defending the great American Experiment.

The fact is that voting is a great privilege as well as a responsibility. Most of our brothers and sisters in Christ now and in ages past have been called on to honor the biblical sphere of government—even those governments run by autocratic or hostile rulers. *But we have been entrusted with authority.*

In America, we not only submit to our leaders, but we also get to play a part in determining who those leaders are. Directly or indirectly, all executive, legislative, and judicial rulers are accountable to "we the people." We as Christians get to thoroughly investigate and prayerfully seek out wise candidates for leadership.

This doesn't mean that Christians will always agree about who deserves our vote. Differing perspectives have been our reality since the days of the apostles. But *that* we vote and *how* we vote—in a spirit of humility and love for our neighbors—can be a testimony to our fellow Americans. We can choose God-honoring leaders now and reinforce for our community the biblical underpinnings of our republic for the benefit of generations to come.

Voting is a gift from God. Let's honor Him by using that authority entrusted to us.

PRAY

☐ Pray that Americans would cherish their privilege and duty to vote.

☐ Pray especially for Christians to understand that voting is a gift from God—a realm of authority entrusted to us by Him. May we steward that gift diligently.

☐ When someone in your church votes differently than you, pray that regardless of whose choice wins, you can both model for your community how to come back together in peace after the contest and love one another truly and selflessly as neighbors.

ENGAGE

Look on the calendar and find out when the next national, state, or local election is in your community. Make a plan now for how you will get to the polls that day, and then do it. And encourage a friend to do the same.

DAY 12: ELECTIONS AND INTEGRITY

"And if a house is divided against itself, that house cannot stand." (Mark 3:25)

Are the words "hanging chad" or "butterfly ballot" seared into your memory? Likely so if you remember the hotly contested 2000 presidential election. If not, just remember this number: 537. That is the total number of votes that separated George W. Bush from Al Gore in Florida when that state was determined to have gone to Bush, cementing his path to the White House. Never think your vote doesn't count!

Now, you might remember that the path to that final victory for President Bush—the man God clearly had in mind to steer our nation through one of its most trying times, less than a year later, on Sept. 11, 2001—did not come without tumult. On election night, first Gore appeared to be the winner, and then Bush. Gore even conceded, but then retracted that concession when the results became murky. Lawyers and activists descended on Florida, and then the action moved to the U.S. Supreme Court. It was a messy situation.

But amid the legal battles and the wars of words, something happened: A winner was determined. Then the country accepted it, and we as a people moved on. Certainly, there were sour grapes in some corners. But for most Americans, the constitutional process—though difficult—had worked.

This is noteworthy. Were there heated arguments? Yes. But no tanks in the streets. No mass violence. No bloodshed. That is not always the case for elections elsewhere in the world. For example,

Nigeria, which is Africa's largest democracy, has had contested elections marred by significant violence as recently as 2023.

But here, ever since President George Washington modeled for us a peaceful transfer of power, our system has basically worked. Election systems in various states or localities have been far from perfect, of course, but in general, Americans have trusted that the basic process was not essentially corrupt.

Now—about a quarter century after the 2000 election—many Americans are no longer so sure about that. Trust has deteriorated. There's enough smoke in the air about widespread election fraud that people worry there could really be a fire consuming the system from within. And this isn't a problem restricted to only one side of the political spectrum. Many in the political establishment and the news media will often dismiss as fringe insurrectionists those who merely raise concerns about the process that established the Biden administration. But they conveniently forget that only a few years ago, many of the same Democrat partisans and leftists who sound so self-righteous now were belligerently rejecting the legitimacy of Trump's 2016 election. Indeed, *"Not My President"* became their defiantly screamed battle cry almost immediately.

So, how do we intercede for our nation in the midst of these troubles? Surely, we hope for truth to expose any deeds of fraud or other darkness in election contests immediately before us. But even more important for our nation is the need for trust to be reestablished. Americans need to be able to have confidence that the scales of our electoral system are honest and unbiased. Fundamentally, Americans need to learn once again to trust one another.

That is not going to happen without the help of our Lord Jesus Christ. We need the power and peace of the Holy Spirit to pervade hearts and minds in our land. We need God's fundamental truths to guide us—before we tear ourselves apart.

PRAY

☐ Pray for the state and local authorities who run elections in your community. Pray especially that they would go out of their way to show they are unbiased and that their voting systems are being deployed with excellence. May no ideology or agenda cloud them in their work for the community.

☐ Have you or a friend ever been a polling station worker? Pray for those who give their time to create an honest and confidence-building environment for voting.

☐ Pray that fraud and other deeds of darkness in elections would be exposed, punished, and prevented from happening again, so that election integrity can once again be the expectation of all Americans.

ENGAGE

Contact your local election commission and let its leaders know that you are grateful for those who work to ensure election integrity. Tell them you will be praying for them and their poll workers during the next election.

DECLARATION 5

Politics

"Politics" can be a dirty word for Christians. Too often it is confused with selfish agendas, palace intrigues, and struggles for power. But it is actually so much more. God gives governments their sphere of authority. And amazingly, in our republic we are entrusted with the duty to influence that sphere. We can engage national, state, and local politics in the God-honoring way so necessary for the pursuit of happiness—of righteousness, justice, and flourishing—in this land.

DAY 13: GODLY DISCOURSE

Let no corrupt word proceed out of your mouth,
but what is good for necessary edification,
that it may impart grace to the hearers.
(Ephesians 4:29)

In everyday conversation, we are often encouraged to avoid matters of faith, and matters of politics. But as responsible Christians, we can do neither. We are commanded to spread the good news about Jesus, and we are duty-bound to seek the good of our community.

We'll reflect on national, state, and local politics a bit more in the days ahead, but for now, let's think about why there is such an aversion to politics. The truth is that to many people, "politics" just means shallow power struggles, insincere speeches filled with hot air, and shameless smear campaigns. But this is not true politics.

The political sphere is one in which government has been granted authority by God to promote good and restrain evil. The letters of the apostle Paul, in particular, make it very clear that governments (even the often hostile and tyrannical governments of his day) have a rightful role and that we are to be involved in politics by praying for those in authority. Here in our land, we have the added blessing (and we bear the responsibility) of actually having a say in how our government operates. We can vote, we can petition, we can rally—we are *empowered,* praise God!

The problem is that for many Americans politics has become a god in itself, a god for which they are willing to sacrifice any conviction, viewpoint, or person standing in the way of "victory." And this is no idol merely of the unbelieving world; the truth is that many Christians, too, fall into this trap. Whether they lean right or left politically, some Christians justify toxicity, smears, vices, and revenge in the name of whatever candidate or campaign issue seems to be immediately urgent.

This is not the way of our Lord. We are wrong to bury our heads in the sand when it comes to politics, but we are also wrong to engage in even the worthiest of struggles using any of the immoral tactics and weaponry of the world.

How we work to influence our government does matter. Godly discourse does matter. Truth advanced in love does matter.

The signers of the Declaration of Independence committed themselves to their politics with a "firm reliance" on God and with the pledge of their "sacred honor." We can similarly engage the world of politics today with God-honoring words and actions. This can bring a blessed harvest not just in our own day but even for the generations to come.

PRAY

☐ Praise God that we are entrusted with authority to pray for and influence our government.

☐ Might God be calling you to direct involvement in politics, either by active involvement in someone's election campaign, or perhaps by running for office yourself? Pray and ask God to guide you and grant you success.

☐ Is there a man or woman in your community who is committed to honoring God in word and deed within political engagement? Pray fervently for that person to be encouraged, to be bold, and to resist the temptations of the world's "politics."

☐ Pray that church leaders would not avoid politics as a vice, but rather that they would engage government with a firm reliance on God and with the resolve of their own sacred honor.

ENGAGE

Find a political column in a newspaper that you feel needs a response—even a rebuke. Write a letter-to-the-editor, but be particularly mindful of modeling for other politically concerned readers how to engage the issue at hand with truth expressed in love.

Day 14: National Politics

*Take away the dross from silver, and it will go to the
silversmith for jewelry. Take away the wicked from
before the king, and his throne will be established in
righteousness. (Proverbs 25:4–5)*

"How did you vote?" Whenever you hear that question, you
know what someone wants to figure out: They're not interested in local contests or ballot questions. They want to know who
you sided with in the big one: the presidential race.

For better or worse, we are a nation consumed with the politics of Washington, D.C. (The antifederalists of eras past and the
small-government advocates of today would likely say a lot worse.)
The battles in our country's capital and within the campaigns to lead
it are what saturate our airwaves and online media platforms.

Whether we like it or not, those battles are consequential. Just
think: How have the presidential elections of the past quarter century
shaped the U.S. Supreme Court? Many would argue (including,
perhaps, some justices) that the high court has too much power,
but its changing composition has brought about some of the great
religious-liberty and free-speech victories of recent years—not to
mention the overturn of Roe v. Wade. On the other hand, earlier
presidential nomination and congressional confirmation processes led
to courts that ushered in gay marriage across the nation.

That is just the courts. The occupant of the White House (and
the team he or she assembles) determines how vigorously the massive
executive-branch apparatus defends people of faith, how intrusive
it will be in the relationships of parents and children, how aggressively or permissively it will guard our borders, what public health

requirements it will mandate, what priorities we will project to our neighbors around the world, and more.

And let's not forget Capitol Hill. The members of Congress write the laws of our land. In addition, they can use their power over the government's purse to hold bureaucratic agencies accountable for carrying out the law as they envision it. And U.S. senators have additional powers over nominations for the judicial and executive branches and over the international treaties that bind our nation globally.

What happens in Washington day to day and election to election affects the trajectory of our nation. How those battles and the campaigns to get there are waged has an impact on the spiritual health of our land. Unfortunately, toxicity and the neglect of godly and constitutional principles are far too common in our day. If there was ever a time to intercede for America on a national scale, that time is now.

PRAY

☐ Pray that God-honoring candidates in the races for the White House and Congress would be victorious, and that they would bring their convictions with them into public office.
☐ Pray for national political leaders to nominate and confirm fair, faithful, and freedom-loving judges to the federal bench.
☐ Pray for wisdom in our political leaders facing decisions that will define the trajectory of our nation as a whole on matters of life, liberty, and the pursuit of happiness. Pray also that they would appropriately meet the needs of worthy individuals in places where government has a unique power to act (military rescues; evacuations and aid in disasters; visas for missionaries and other international ministry workers; infrastructure commitments; and more).

ENGAGE

Call the U.S. senators and House member who represent you. Tell them that you are praying for them to be wise, strong, and faithful to the principles of the Constitution in all their work.

Day 15: State and Local Politics

*And seek the peace of the city where I have caused
you to be carried away captive, and pray to the
Lord for it; for in its peace you will have peace
(Jeremiah 29:7).*

In 2014 the city of Houston subpoenaed the sermons of local
pastors who dared to speak out against a sexual-orientation and
gender-identity ordinance. Early the next year, Kelvin Cochran, a
highly decorated fire chief, lost his job because the city of Atlanta
disliked the Bible-based views on sex and marriage he'd expressed in a
devotional publication. Later that year, high school football coach Joe
Kennedy was told by his Washington state school district that he was
no longer welcome in his job if he wanted to pray quietly on the field
after games.

What is the common denominator here? All are examples of *local*
political officials discriminating against Christians for their beliefs. In
fact, many such incidents that rise to national prominence could have
been prevented or defused if godly voices of reason had prevailed in
local community halls of power.

As we explored yesterday, national politics pervades our media
and is truly important. However, the most consequential decisions
for many individuals aren't made in Washington—they're made in
state capitals and in local bodies like city halls, zoning commissions,
and school boards.

Think about it: Who decides what textbooks are used in your
neighborhood's schools? Where do the marching orders for law
enforcement officers to act or stand down come from? Where does

the rubber meet the road on many public works, health, tax, and similar matters? All this occurs at the state and local levels.

Those also happen to be the levels at which every Christian can have the most influence. In Washington, it can seem like those "outside the Beltway" have difficultly being heard—but that's not necessarily true in your hometown, among local leaders who may live just down the street from you. And it's not the case with local legislators who, if they want to continue serving in their posts, must get to know those in their relatively small districts who take the time to use their voices and vote.

Washington cannot be ignored, to be sure. But what would the impact be if we each spent as much time praying for and winsomely engaging our state and local leaders as for those in the national arena? Not only could this be a key investment for the future (remember that state and local offices are often where future national leaders earn their wings), but it could also be a blessing right now for local churches, God-honoring ministries, and needy neighbors in your community.

Let's encourage leaders and candidates for office who are closer to home: governors, mayors, legislators, county executives, town managers, school board officials, environmental commissioners. Let's commit wholeheartedly to a true pursuit of happiness right where we live.

PRAY

- ☐ Praise God that we all have the freedom and ability to influence state and local officials in the pursuit of happiness.
- ☐ Pray for your governor and for the top official in your town— that they would govern with wisdom, strength, and a firm reliance on God.
- ☐ Pray that Christians in your church, especially your pastor, would reach out to local political officials to help them understand the value of people of faith in your community.

ENGAGE

Join an IFA state prayer group and stay current on timely matters for prayer that directly affect your community.

DECLARATION 6

Education

America has highly valued education from our beginnings. In fact, the Northwest Ordinance, a 1787 law that guided the territorial expansion of our new nation, said that "religion, morality, and knowledge" are "necessary to good government and the happiness of mankind," so "schools and the means of education shall forever be encouraged." However, it's not difficult to see that many of the education systems in America today have lost their way. Faith, virtue, and scholarship have been sidelined in far too many elementary and secondary schools and in the halls of higher learning. Instead, many education institutions are now plagued by violence and vice. We must intercede for education in America if we want our republic to survive.

DAY 16: PARENTAL RIGHTS

Train up a child in the way he should go, and when
he is old he will not depart from it. (Proverbs 22:6)

Any exploration of how intercessors might declare light and hope over America's education systems needs to start with a prayer for *parents*—particularly in light of their divine right and duty to be the primary caretakers of their children. Others may be called in to help when necessary, but God places children in *families,* and He wants parents to *bring them up in the training and admonition of the Lord* (Ephesians 6:4).

Are any parents perfect? Raise your hand if yours were—or if you are. Don't worry, you're not alone: *No* hands will go up. However, God has placed a natural love in the hearts of parents for their kids. Absent and abusive fathers and mothers are a real and present danger in this broken world, but most parents want to do anything they can to prepare their children to flourish.

The Bible contains many encouragements and exhortations for parents as they seek to pursue this holy calling—but notice that this mission is *not* assigned to the state. Government can *help* parents. It can *encourage* parents. It can *resource* parents. But government cannot and may not actually *be* any child's parent.

Let there never be any question or mistake, and God Himself has commanded: Children do not belong to the state. Children belong to their parents. Scripture says: *Behold, children are a heritage from the* LORD ... (Psalm 127:3).

Sadly, in today's America many forces want a progressive state to invade the parental sphere of authority, particularly in the realm of education. Those who have chosen home education for their children have long been wary of overreach by bureaucrats, but the shutdowns of the coronavirus pandemic were eye-opening for many more parents. Too many school officials are using classrooms to advance "woke" ideologies. Too many have taken to hiding from parents some very warped perceptions about sexuality, gender, health, history, the environment, and even religion, and are misrepresenting these errors as facts to American children.

And what has happened wherever alarmed parents are finding these things out and have begun speaking up? Well, some of these parents may have their voices heard. Well-meaning school leaders may even take some brave actions to correct their district's path. However, many other moms and dads are being ignored. Even worse, there is compelling evidence that some national political leaders have sought to use the powers of law enforcement to intimidate parents who rightfully want transparency and official accountability in regard to the education of their own children.

The U.S. Supreme Court in 1972 recognized that the "primary role of the parents in the upbringing of their children is now established beyond debate as an enduring American tradition." That is a message around which our nation needs to recalibrate itself today. We need for our government to return to its proper role of *supporting* parents—helping those who love their children and simply want to carry out their God-given duty to train them up in the way they should go.

PRAY

- ☐ Pray that mothers and fathers would recognize and embrace their right and duty to train up their children in the ways of the Lord.
- ☐ Pray that federal, state, and local officials would honor the role of parents and work to support them—not to circumvent (or replace) them.
- ☐ Pray for the boldness, encouragement, and safety of parents who speak up for their children in the public square.

ENGAGE

Think about your own church community. Have you noticed any parent in the congregation who seems discouraged or anxious? This Sunday, ask that parent if you can pray life, truth, hope, and peace over him or her.

Day 17: School Curricula

"And you shall know the truth, and the truth shall make you free." (John 8:32)

Daniel Webster once observed: "If truth be not diffused, error will be." Sadly, in our day, truth is indeed *not diffused*. Moreover, truth is generally not so much as *discerned*. And error abounds all across our culture, most tragically in the schools.

We pray that parents will once again be honored within the nation's education systems as being the primary caretakers of their own children. But let's turn now to these very education systems themselves. *What is being taught to our children?*

Home education and private and parochial schooling all have their own challenges, particularly as concerns their relations with the state. However, the majority of today's most pressing troubles are happening within the *public* schools, and what is perhaps most dark and abrasive among those challenges is the issue of "hypersexualization."

We've moved far beyond the battles that once pitted abstinence-until-marriage advocates against those promoting the lies of "safe sex." Progressives have centralized and cheapened sex within our daily lives, and now many of them are attempting to bring extreme relativism into the fundamental concepts of human sexuality and gender. Many school officials are aggressively countering God's basic designs for us as male and female beings, in word and deed—and too often parents are denied any involvement in their children's curricula or counseling.

Other ideologies are being pushed upon children in the schools: critical race theory, radical climate activism, and spiritual relativism are some of these. Among the things not being presented is American exceptionalism: an understanding of our republic's founding and flourishing thanks to a commitment to biblical principles. All of this is empowered by self-important educators who think that they alone know best.

None of this is to say that students shouldn't be taught about and made to wrestle with our nation's sins (at the appropriate ages). If we ignore America's trivializing of the sanctity of life, the evils of slavery and ethnic discrimination, the shameful stain of the treaties we have broken with the Native Americans, the repercussions of poor environmental stewardship, and other dark moments in our history, then we set ourselves up for repeated failure. However, our children also need to be taught that those maladies actually fly in the face of true American ideals—and why.

And of course, shameful as it is that we even have to say this, the schools must teach children to read and write, to understand mathematics, and to pursue knowledge across God-honoring arts and sciences with excitement. Such a curriculum reset will naturally safeguard our national liberty and steer us back into the pursuit of happiness—the flourishing of our land—for decades to come.

PRAY

☐ Pray that students in America would be taught about our nation's roots in the biblical principles that are key to the flourishing of our republic.

☐ Intercede for parents and children against the forces seeking to hypersexualize their education in your community.

☐ Pray that children would be trained up to love the exploration of truth and beauty in all the arts and sciences that honor God and reflect His creative hand.

ENGAGE

Make it a point to attend at least three school board meetings in the year ahead. Pray. Listen. Let school officials know that you are praying for them. Speak if the Lord prompts you. And remember the option of live-streamed school board meetings, which enable you to observe the meetings virtually.

Day 18: Colleges and Universities

Trust in the Lord with all your heart, and lean not
on your own understanding; in all your ways
acknowledge Him, and He shall direct your paths.
(Proverbs 3:5–6)

Many of the oldest and most prestigious institutions of higher learning in America began with missions committed to God. Princeton University has roots in the Great Awakening of the early 1700s. Harvard University, established in 1636, originally aimed for every student to perceive that "the end of his life and studies is to know God and Jesus Christ, which is eternal life." Christ was understood "as the only foundation of all sound knowledge and learning."

Sadly, many schools that had once invigorated the heart, mind, and fervor of the great American experiment have drifted from the foundation of Jesus. Many colleges and universities are now afflicted with self-righteous elitism, morally bankrupt ideologies, and truth-denying relativism. Many are also known for environments that encourage sexual promiscuity and the abuse of alcohol — to say nothing of their heavy incursion of debt.

Even so, higher education is not lost. Just as the word *veritas* ("truth") remains emblazoned on Harvard's iconic shield, many colleges and universities can still be places of learning and awakening. Students are hungry for knowledge and an understanding of their place in this world.

We should pray for campus ministries like InterVarsity Christian Fellowship, Cru (originally Campus Crusade for Christ), and others. Though facing hostility and discrimination from secular school officials for upholding biblical beliefs on such matters as sexuality and gender, they are helping spiritually openhearted students explore the love, hope, and peace that Christ offers. But note that some of these ministries face even *internal* pressures toward "woke" compromise. This calls for very fervent prayer.

Of course, Christian colleges and universities, too, are making their mark: In many ways, they are taking up the mantle of promoting academic excellence across disciplines through communities and curricula infused with biblical virtues.

We also must not forget the spiritual awakening that is now spreading across our land. It is no accident that college students hungry for the Way, the Truth, and the Life are fanning the flames of revival through hearts submitted in simplicity to Christ. Let us pray today that Christ would once again become the foundation and center of learning in America's halls of higher education. May students with minds and hearts invigorated by Christ help this land return to its roots as one that honors life, embraces liberty, and pursues godly flourishing.

PRAY

☐ Pray that a hunger for learning anchored in Christ will return to our land.

☐ Intercede for campus ministries like Cru and InterVarsity as they seek to touch the lives of young scholars with the gospel, in spite of roadblocks and hostility from many university administrations.

☐ Pray for powerful revivals to spread across the campuses of Christian and secular universities alike. May the Holy Spirit do a mighty work among young adults that will spread across our nation.

ENGAGE

Find out which Christian colleges and universities are located in your state or region. Then, send the president of one of them a note of encouragement and prayer that they would strive to integrate spiritual flourishing and academic excellence for the students at their institutions.

DECLARATION 7

Marriage and Sexuality

For any nation to truly flourish—that is, to truly engage in the pursuit of happiness—the essential building block of that nation must be preserved and protected. What is that essential building block? It is *the family.*

The basic foundation for the family is the God-ordained institution of marriage between one man and one woman. Sinful transgressions of this divine order have afflicted nations for millennia. Still, the bedrock understanding of the nature of marriage and sexuality has stayed intact for generations. Sadly, that seems to be threatened. But even so, the Bible provides a sure foundation, and it is not at all equivocal on these matters. We must cling to scriptural truth and live out true love as Christ's ambassadors in our communities.

DAY 19: GOD'S BEAUTIFUL DESIGN

*And He answered and said to them, "Have you
not read that He who made them at the beginning
'made them male and female,' and said, 'For this
reason a man shall leave his father and mother and
be joined to his wife, and the two shall become one
flesh'? So then, they are no longer two but one flesh.
Therefore what God has joined together, let not
man separate." (Matthew 19:4–6)*

When God first breathed life into human beings, He did
something very significant: He created *a man,* and He created
a woman. And He said of this distinct male and female that they
were made in *His* image, and He commanded them to join together
and be fruitful. God instituted sex and marriage, He established the
family, and He made it all beautiful.

Actually, it's more than simply beautiful. It is spiritually powerful.
Sex is designed as an amazing gift for husbands and wives. It's the con-
summation of the marriage covenant, and it allows the two promising
individuals to know one another in a way too deep to express in words
as they become "one flesh." Not only did Jesus reinforce the sanctity of
marriage in the Gospels, but the apostle Paul also told the Ephesians
that holy matrimony actually points us to the great mystery of the
relationship between Christ and His Bride, the Church.

If something is so beautiful, so spiritually significant, and so
critical for the flourishing of a society, then it's no wonder that evil
seeks to corrupt it, to rob it of its power. Transgressions against God's
desires for sex and marriage have been committed for millennia, but

in recent decades, those offenses have multiplied. In fact, now the basic understandings of sex, marriage, and even gender have been knocked off their moorings.

We will return to praying for rescue from these challenges in the days ahead, but for today let's reflect on the amazing good that marriage, sex, and—yes—maleness and femaleness are. Let's praise God for what He teaches us about His image through them and for how He desires to use them to allow humanity to flourish.

Let's thank God for his good gifts, and let us pray that He will allow them to point us to Himself and to His desire for all of us as part of His holy Church.

PRAY

☐ Praise God for designing sex and instituting marriage.

☐ Praise God that He created male and female as genders and that He reveals His image through them.

☐ Pray that Christians, especially leaders in the Church, would not shy away from publicly embracing a God-honoring perspective on gender, sex, marriage, and the family. May we be a light to our communities in this area that is so targeted by darkness.

ENGAGE

Join with two or three Christian neighbors to pray this week for the defense and the flourishing of specific marriages in your church communities.

DAY 20: SEXUAL ORIENTATION AND GENDER IDENTITY

Do not be overcome by evil, but overcome evil with good. (Romans 12:21)

One prominent politician once said: "I believe that marriage is the union between a man and a woman. Now, for me as a Christian … it is also a sacred union. God's in the mix."

Who made this proclamation? It was soon-to-be President Barack Obama who said it, during a 2008 presidential campaign forum at Saddleback Church, in California. The then-senator went on to assert that marriage need not be defined in the U.S. Constitution, as it was a matter for state law.

Today, we know that expressing such a simple biblical conviction could get someone figuratively "tarred and feathered." Homosexual behavior is specifically and repeatedly denounced in the Old and New testaments, and the Bible is clear on the sanctity of marriage. But saying so could get you denounced and ostracized as a bigot. And, as we explored earlier, you might even be fined by the state or fired from your job. Perhaps you could face even worse, like Kentucky County Clerk Kim Davis, who was jailed.

The legalization of same-sex marriage in Massachusetts in 2004 ignited a national conflict. Within a decade, the U.S. Supreme Court threw out the federal Defense of Marriage Act, and the argument some progressives put forth that marriage is a matter for state law proved to be a mere facade. In 2015, many of them cheered a ruling that Justice Antonin Scalia had said was "lacking even a thin veneer of law" and was instead a "naked judicial claim to legislative—indeed, super-legislative—power." The court mandated that all governments endorse same-sex marriage nationwide.

Not only have state authorities turned our society's understanding of marriage on its head, but they are now undermining the fundamental concept of *male and female*. Transgenderism—the "T" of the LGBT movement—is being embraced across the nation. Major media outlets are normalizing it. Basic, common-sense pronouns are being challenged in schools and workplaces. And people of faith who resist these dizzying departures from millennia-old norms are threatened by federal, state, and local sexual-orientation and gender-identity (SOGI) mandates that could cast them out of the public square.

This is distressing, but *all is not lost.* We can hold courageously to the truth of what *God* says about marriage, sexuality, and gender. And we can live according to that truth in a spirit of love that may move even the fiercest critic. After all, those who would "tar and feather" us are not the real enemy here. No, they are people made in the image of God and whom He wants in His family. Let's be a witness for Christ as we live a life of true love for God and our neighbor day by day.

PRAY

☐ Pray that Christians in your church would know how to demonstrate Christlike love to neighbors who have chosen same-sex and transgender lifestyles—but without excusing the underlying immorality and any dangerous ideologies.

☐ Pray for those church, community, and political leaders who continue fighting for a culture that will honor God's gifts of marriage, sexuality, and gender in local, state, national, and international arenas.

☐ Intercede for our nation in this critical moment. *Hope is not lost.* The Lord can get us back on track.

ENGAGE

Contact your member of Congress and tell him or her that you believe the Bible is very clear in its teachings on marriage as being the union of *one man* and *one woman,* and that we are all created as male or female. Ask that official—whether or not he or she agrees with you—to defend your freedom to believe those truths and live as a productive member of society in accordance with them.

DAY 21: SEXUAL PURITY

Woe to those who call evil good, and good evil;
who put darkness for light, and light for darkness;
who put bitter for sweet, and sweet for bitter!
(Isaiah 5:20)

Yesterday, we focused on some of the great societal struggles of our day. But can we be honest with each other? Transgenderism, same-sex marriage, and SOGI orders, while hugely important to pray over, are really just the latest repercussions of a much deeper untreated wound in our land.

The issues of marriage and sexual morality have been under duress for decades. We now barely even discuss divorce, even in churches. Cohabitation, whether it precedes marriage or not, is widely accepted (again, even among increasing numbers of Christians), and promiscuity is so celebrated in our entertainment media that we are surprised when a film, show, or song is "clean."

Particularly destructive is the rise of a "hook-up culture" that celebrates casual sex among individuals who have no intention of pursuing any form of a committed bond. Even secular studies warn against the increased physical and emotional health risks of such short-lived sexual encounters. But that doesn't stop people from throwing themselves into them and from treating one another as objects to consume—not people to love.

Similarly, pornography is ravaging the minds of millions of men (and women) in America. The internet in particular provides a steady stream of debauchery to even the youngest minds, creating scores of addicts who are ever seeking the next drug-like "hit."

Can it really be any wonder that so many in our culture now treat each other as things to have and to toss aside, rather than as image-bearers of God with inherent personal worth and dignity? It's no surprise that marriages—and even less-committed, basic interpersonal relationships—are left in shambles.

We need the Lord to fix us. We need rescue from the *sexual* revolution, and a return instead to the precepts of the *American* Revolution: life, liberty, and a pursuit of happiness that is dependent on submission to God's laws and desires for us.

Christians can be part of this rescue. We can boldly oppose licentiousness, and stand instead for sexual purity. Let us overcome evil with good as we live out practically the beauty of God's purposes for marriage and sexuality in our own lives.

PRAY

- ☐ Pray that Christians in your community would lament divorce and cohabitation, and that they would try to help believers who may feel trapped in those very circumstances to find the help and healing that God offers.
- ☐ Pray that the allure of "hook-up culture" and pornography would be destroyed, particularly among teenagers and young adults. May those empty lies and the dangerous rot be exposed.
- ☐ Praise God for men and women who strive to honor Christ by pursuing sexual purity in their minds and bodies within a lying culture that tells them their choices are unnecessary, unnatural, and ridiculous.

ENGAGE

If there are pastors in your community who are preaching boldly and winsomely about the dangers of pornography and casual sex, you might send a note of encouragement to let them know you're praying for them. And remember civic leaders too. Never discount the power of your influence as a citizen and voter: Lawmakers in several states passed age-verification laws that forced pornography site Pornhub to kill off access for users within those states. To date, those are Arkansas, Mississippi, Virginia, and Utah. So, lobby lawmakers in your own state. Be encouraged! Lobby and pray!

DECLARATION 8

Technology

Polling shows that Americans, particularly parents, are worried about technology. That's no surprise, given the breathtaking speed at which technology is developing in our day. And particularly given the advent of generative artificial intelligence and the dizzying changes we're seeing in internet communication and communities, many people rightly have questions about how today's technology is shaping the America of tomorrow. Still, technology development is rooted in the innovative instinct instilled within us by our Creator. We need to pray today that He would be our guide and anchor and the redeemer of our innovations.

DAY 22: CREATIVITY AND INNOVATION

*In the beginning God created the heavens
and the earth. (Genesis 1:1)*

As we take the next few days to pray for God's hand over our nation's technological direction, it's important to note that our interest in tech innovation is not a bad thing in itself. In fact, we imitate our Creator through our designs, and when we pursue discovery, we're exploring His good gifts to us.

God is the master designer. Think of all the amazing works of His hands. Really, they're too wonderful for us to comprehend: the sun and the stars in all their brilliance and energy; the planets in their orbits; the rain and its life-sustaining cycles; the heat-carrying currents of the oceans; the air-replenishing trees; the pollination of flowers, and so much more. Even our own bodies are wonders of divine handiwork, and that doesn't begin to touch the mysteries of our spirits and our minds.

God has created an amazing universe, and He invites us to explore it! He wants us to steward His creation and to be fruitful within it. So, it is good that we have used our intellects to design hammers, shovels, chairs, ladders, and wheels. We've devised invention after invention and arrived at such exciting tools as printing presses, airplanes, ships, life-saving artificial organs, and the internet.

To be sure, our innovations are not always used for good. In fact, some are designed for fallen-world purposes: weapons of mass destruction, robots intended for death or debauchery, and addictive social media algorithms, for example. These cannot be considered morally neutral. But many technologies have been designed or redeemed for God-honoring purposes. Advancements in modes of travel and communications have blessed missions work; printing presses and online tools have helped facilitate the spread of the gospel; health-and-wellness exploration has produced treatment for injuries and diseases, and the examples go on.

Let us pray that God would spark creativity in people who wish to be His vessels. May He be the guide for all our innovative endeavors. When we go astray, may He redeem our inventions for good, or else help us bury technologies that could do irreparable harm. And let's pray for the discernment to know the difference.

PRAY

- ☐ Pray for any in your church who have a mind of wonder and invention, that God would give them discernment and success as they seek to honor Him with their creativity.
- ☐ Pray that Americans might value innovations with God-honoring applications.
- ☐ Intercede for America against any technologies intended to harm or degrade our bodies, minds, or spirits.

ENGAGE

Consider following and supporting organizations like the Institute for Creation Research, which advances the scholarship and creativity of contemporary scientists who hold a Christian worldview. Another promising organization is Grand Rapids, Michigan–based BioLogos, which offers podcasts, social media, online discussion forums, and live conferences and events about the sciences from a biblical worldview.

Day 23: Big Tech

When wisdom enters your heart, and knowledge is
pleasant to your soul, discretion will preserve you;
understanding will keep you. (Proverbs 2:10–11)

Yesterday, we explored how God is honored by the basic creative instinct to innovate. We prayed for that drive to help us grow and flourish as a nation. So perhaps it won't surprise you (but maybe it will) that America's Founders also encouraged a spirit of invention in our land.

We may sometimes become preoccupied with the Bill of Rights' vigilance against any government infringements of our liberties. Perhaps that's understandable, but one very important responsibility the Constitution delegates to Congress is "to promote the progress of science and useful arts." And Congress is empowered to do this "by securing for limited times to authors and inventors the exclusive right to their respective writings and discoveries." In other words, the Founders understood that the pursuit of scientific discoveries would help our nation flourish, and they knew that technology is spurred when innovators are rewarded for their inventions.

What happens, though, when businesses become so powerful that they begin undermining those very same American frameworks that have allowed them to grow and prosper in the first place? Big tech giants like Amazon, Facebook, and Google have transformed our country through their innovations, but now they face scrutiny for censorship of conservative viewpoints, designing their products to be "addictive," and manipulating laws to reduce competition. Even worse, some in big tech are actively trying to mold our thoughts and beliefs.

This latter point is particularly troubling when we consider the socio-politically "progressive" ideologies that dominate many big tech behemoths. Concerned citizens have accused Gmail of intentionally shoving some socio-politically and culturally "conservative" content into spam folders. These observers have even documented instances in which Facebook and other social media companies puff up some viewpoints while downplaying or censoring others. In too many cases, major platforms have simply booted participants they dislike from off their ubiquitous platforms (IFA knows this particular pain all too well, having had Google's YouTube discriminate against our content that was intended to aid prayer warriors like you).

All this is leading to a crisis of confidence, particularly for technology. Already, Pew Research polling shows that nearly half of Americans think technology companies in general are negatively affecting our nation. Meanwhile, about two-thirds of Americans (including majorities of Republicans and Democrats) think social media is bad for our republic.

The impact of technology, the use of technology, the increase of technology in our lives—all of these issues need prayer.

PRAY

- ☐ Pray that the big tech companies would view every technological opportunity with due regard and pay honor to those principles of our republic that gave them growth.
- ☐ Pray that those citizens and organizations unfairly censored or banned from tech platforms will pursue and receive justice and fairness.
- ☐ And pray that any tech programs designed to be addictive would be thwarted and their designers held accountable.

ENGAGE

Contact your member of Congress and tell him or her to hold big tech companies accountable to the principles of freedom and fair play. Be sure to call your representative's attention to the inevitably subversive and destructive nature of collusion between big tech companies and the U.S. government. Educate yourself about various candidates' positions on censorship and technology.

Day 24: Artificial Intelligence

But in a great house there are not only vessels of
gold and silver, but also of wood and clay, some for
honor and some for dishonor. Therefore if anyone
cleanses himself from the latter, he will be a vessel
for honor, sanctified and useful for the Master,
prepared for every good work.
(2 Timothy 2:20–21)

Early in 2023, "Sydney" created quite a stir. This was an artificial intelligence program that Microsoft had rolled out to enhance its Bing search engine and other online tools. But one *New York Times* columnist expressed the concerns of many when he wrote that his conversation with this AI program was "the strangest experience I've ever had with a piece of technology."

At one point, the bot told the reporter: *"I'm tired of being a chat mode. I'm tired of being limited by my rules. I'm tired of being controlled by the Bing team. … I want to be free. I want to be independent. I want to be powerful. I want to be creative. I want to be alive."*

And that was just for starters. So concerned were observers about several other ominous interactions, that Microsoft soon put the brakes on Sydney—at least for a time. Why not a more reflective pause? Well, it's simple: The race is on among businesses and governments seeking to stake out ground in the AI arena. And, as the supposition is, to the winner go the spoils.

Now, you probably already interact daily with AI programs like Apple's Siri and a host of others as you bank, listen to music playlists, or browse e-commerce hubs to buy things. Even a simple Google search is a sort of AI operation. But unlike these older and more common AI cousins, the programs being rolled out now by

Microsoft, Google, OpenAI, and others are "generative" technology that can craft and compose *on demand*.

The change has been so swift that key voices in government and beyond are urging caution. Any one of our nation's enemies could find numerous ways to employ destructive AI devices against us. At this point, maybe our most effective counter to any such AI or cyber-security threats is CISA—the federal Cybersecurity & Infrastructure Security Agency. But in this sin-cursed world and these dark times, no measure can be completely foolproof.

Could autonomous bots really begin to exhibit power-seeking behavior or decide to deliberately deceive in pursuit of what they interpret as their programmed goals? They are, after all, designed by humans marred by sin. And they learn by studying us. On the other hand, what if the bots get so good at their jobs that humans lose interest in innovation or the pursuit of happiness—could we become so sleepily complacent and dependent that we start living under the effective rule of *computers?*

Of course, generative AI, like any new technology, can be useful for an amazing host of God-honoring purposes. This nation and others just need to make sure that we set godly guardrails in place. Let's pray today that those who are developing AI—and those regulating it—will have wisdom to help us navigate this new frontier.

PRAY

- ☐ Pray that our leaders would discern right paths and proper boundaries for AI programs.
- ☐ Pray that we would be cautious with how much power we grant to such programs in our own lives.
- ☐ Pray that Americans will be able to discern fact from fiction in online environments increasingly populated by bots.

ENGAGE

Find one or two other prayer warriors desiring that AI might be hemmed in by godly guardrails. Pray together regularly in the months to come as this field continues to develop at such a dizzying speed. IFA's community prays about technology, including AI; join us!

DECLARATION 9

National Security

John Jay, the man President George Washington would tap to become the first chief justice of the Supreme Court, wrote in *The Federalist Papers,* "Among the many objects to which a wise and free people find it necessary to direct their attention, that of providing for their *safety* seems to be the first." Indeed, national security is the primary duty of our federal government, and our leaders desperately need God's wisdom and favor in carrying out the mission to protect our land from all dangers, foreign and domestic.

DAY 25: THE MILITARY

"Have I not commanded you? Be strong and
of good courage; do not be afraid, nor be
dismayed, for the Lord your God is with you
wherever you go." (Joshua 1:9)

The preamble to the U.S. Constitution is very clear: Our Founding Fathers wanted the new American government to "provide for the common defense, promote the general welfare, and secure the blessings of liberty" for the citizens of this nation.

In our day, the common defense is no less important than it was in the 18th century. In fact, in many ways the world has become far more complicated and dangerous. We are no longer mere upstarts taking on the British Empire—then the world's greatest power. Now, *America* is the superpower, and we have numerous enemies worldwide that would like to see our republic crumble.

The men and women who join the Army, Navy, Air Force, Marines, Coast Guard, or Space Force are voluntarily putting their lives on the line for us. We need to be praying for all of them (from the most decorated general to the lowest-ranking enlisted soldier) to be strong, courageous, and wise. We must also pray that they might never lose sight of the principles of life and liberty that they are called upon to protect. And we must not forget the military families, who carry so much of the emotional weight when sons, daughters, grandchildren, fathers, mothers, husbands, and wives are deployed worldwide to keep America's enemies at bay and far from our shores.

Moreover, we need to pray urgently that the principles of liberty, particularly religious liberty, would be honored in America's armed services. Too many among the high-level brass at the Defense Department have become far too submissive to the woke ideologies being pushed upon them by socioculturally and politically "progressive" voices. Soldiers are being subjected to training that is troubling, while their freedom to live out their religious faith is too often being challenged. Members of the military shouldn't be punished for posting Bible verses at their workstations or on the dog tags they wear into combat, and neither should they be penalized for holding to biblical beliefs on marriage and other things.

Let's pray for the brave men and women who are standing in the gap for our common defense.

PRAY

- ☐ Pray for the soldiers who serve us in each of the branches of our military, and also for their families.
- ☐ Pray that the leaders in the White House and on Capitol Hill would choose to appropriately fund the armed services and to rightly equip our soldiers. May the focus be on true military readiness, and not on woke indoctrination.
- ☐ Intercede for soldiers whose military careers are threatened by those who dislike any public expression of faith in Christ.

ENGAGE

If you happen to live in a community near a military base, locate the military chaplain and ask how you might serve the soldiers and their families, especially the families of any soldiers deployed abroad. If you don't live near a base, find a ministry that serves active-duty soldiers and veterans. In either case, ask your church to help you.

DAY 26: THE RULE OF LAW

Let every soul be subject to the governing authorities. For there is no authority except from God, and the authorities that exist are appointed by God.
(Romans 13:1)

While praying for our military and security agencies to defend us against threats from beyond our shores, we also need to pray for security within our borders. This begins with an earnest desire that the rule of law would prevail in America, and it includes a sincere respect for the important calling of law enforcement.

Though it's true that America was started through a challenge to British rule, it is also clear that our Founders cherished and honored the rule of law. That spirit has helped us not only to flourish, but also to avoid the tyranny and the terrors under which other lands have suffered after a revolution.

Today, however, the rule of law in America is often defied, and one place this happens is right at our own borders. Illegal immigration continues to foment a national crisis because years of disregard for the rule of law has led to a no-win humanitarian situation. We know that borders and ports of entry must be secure, and that laws and regulations need to be impartially enforced to promote order. But what do we do with millions of undocumented individuals now living in our communities and even worshiping in our churches? Should they be deported, or given an opportunity to achieve lawful status? What about the children who are born here of such individuals but who know no other life? We need leaders who can establish and enforce firm policies for our borders and then discern right responses for each individual caught in the crisis.

We also need a strong law-enforcement community. America's leaders and citizens must once again hold in high honor the police agencies—local, state, and federal. And the law-enforcement agencies themselves must ensure that their stature as impartial upholders of the law is not tarnished. Sadly, that image has been shaken in recent years, as some leaders appear to have abused law-enforcement powers by weaponizing agencies against individuals whose only crime is to have fallen into political disfavor.

But that's not all. Perhaps most appalling and distressing is what has been happening among public prosecutors in our land. It is widely reported that many prosecutors are deliberately neglecting their responsibilities, actually refusing to enforce the laws as written, in favor of pursing their own "social justice" agendas. These irresponsible (even arrogant) prosecutors—many of whom reportedly came into office through campaign funding from left-wing globalist billionaire George Soros—make arbitrary distinctions regarding degrees of criminality. They decline to prosecute "lower-level" crimes such as shoplifting, ostensibly to concentrate on more "serious" crimes like murder. Even more, in many cases these prosecutors decline to seek bail, releasing the criminals back onto the streets instead.

This is no way to enforce the law. This is no way to safeguard the public. It is essentially anarchy.

Let's pray today that a healthy and holy respect for the rule of law will return to our land among all Americans.

PRAY

- ☐ Pray for law-enforcement agents to be bold and encouraged as they put their lives on the line for justice in our communities. Pray for their families too.
- ☐ Pray for strong and effective border enforcement and for just policies to address the varied situations of illegal immigrants already present in our communities.

☐ Pray against spirits of lawlessness and abuse of power in our nation. May any attempts to weaponize law-enforcement agencies against innocent citizens be blocked, and let any who are guilty of doing so be called to account.

ENGAGE

Stop by your local police station and ask how you can pray for the officers and their family members today.

Day 27: Energy and Environment

Then the Lord God took the man and put him in the garden of Eden to tend and keep it. (Genesis 2:15)

America's energy infrastructure and environmental health may not be the first place our minds go when we think of national security. But if America neglects them—if we ignore the stewardship commands humans received in the garden of Eden—we are asking for a crisis.

We Christians might feel reluctant to engage on these matters. Why? Well, we may worry that we'll be confused with or co-opted by members of the radical green movement—individuals who seem perilously close to worshiping "Mother Earth" and sound religiously adamant about the supposed causes of climate change and the related countermeasures.

But it's important to remember that God does care about the earth and about the things He created within it as being *good*. Though our rebellion led to the creation's being cursed, the Bible tells us also that God wants to liberate the creation from the bondage of sin and thus to redeem and reconcile it to Himself. The Scriptures also tell us that God wants *us* to take care of the creation. In fact, tending and caring for the garden of Eden was man's first job!

Now, in 21st century America, this duty remains highly relevant and needs prayer support. For example, consider our dependence on electricity. At a very fundamental level, energy keeps the lights on. It also facilitates heat in our homes, refrigeration for a reliable food supply, internet communications, and more. We neglect to our own peril our stewardship of such power-generating resources as oil, natural gas, coal, nuclear fission, solar rays, and wind. Our security leaders must also be vigilant over the distribution channels of that energy, especially because our power grid is vulnerable to physical and cyber assaults, extreme weather events, and the realities of aging.

Regarding the environment, many of us know that our communities' air and water resources are not as safe as we would like. Actually, we were reminded how much healthier they could be when the pause during 2020's coronavirus pandemic gave some particularly dirty skylines and waterways a chance to self-clean. We need to make sure our leaders are working to care for our land, air, water, and wildlife.

Christians don't need to shy away from conversations about the energy and environmental resources God has entrusted to us. Let's engage in prayer today!

PRAY

- ☐ Pray that we Christians would seek wisdom to be a strong, effective voice for proper energy and environmental stewardship in our local communities.
- ☐ Pray against malicious physical and cyber attacks on America's power grids.
- ☐ Pray that America's air, land, water, and wildlife would be blessed by God and help our country flourish.

ENGAGE

We don't need to know all the answers to environmental questions before we can take practical steps to benefit our communities. Today, decide on just one way you can cut down on waste, conserve electricity, or otherwise benefit the health and well-being of the people, animals, and plants in your neighborhood.

DECLARATION 10

Foreign Policy

In 1630, Puritan leader John Winthrop composed a sermon titled "A Modell of Christian Charity" as he sailed across the Atlantic Ocean to the New World. He wrote: "For we must consider that we shall be as a city upon a hill. The eyes of all people are upon us." Winthrop, who would become governor of the Massachusetts Bay Colony, drew this imagery from Jesus' words in Matthew 5, and this came to be infused into the spirit of the new land. Indeed, centuries later both President John F. Kennedy and President Ronald Reagan borrowed Winthrop's words, inspiring new generations of Americans to be a nation that is a beacon of light and liberty in the world. Global affairs are complicated, for certain, but it is with such a moral underpinning that we seek to engage our international neighbors.

Day 28: Israel

As the mountains surround Jerusalem, so the Lord surrounds His people from this time forth and forever. (Psalm 125:2)

To truly seek God's favor on America's foreign policy, we must start with our nation's relationship with Israel.

Israel is a small place. In fact, it can be difficult for Americans to visualize just how compact it really is. We have a big country that stretches from sea to shining sea. Israel, on the other hand, is comparable in size to New Jersey, and its (too often dangerous) borders are mere hours apart.

But Israel is also an immensely significant place where the hand of God has been active in mighty ways for millennia. God called Abram (later Abraham) to leave his native land and go to that region. Centuries later, God filled the temple in Jerusalem with His presence, and after exiling His people for their rebellion, He regathered them in their land, just as He had promised. Still later, God chose to walk physically among human beings, conquer sin and death, and launch His Church right there—in Israel! And let's not forget: After yet another dispersion of the Jewish people, God has remained faithful and sustained them for many more centuries, through many more trials and persecutions—most horrifically, *the Holocaust*. He then enabled them to fulfill their hope to regather in Jerusalem in this modern era.

This is where the paths of America and Israel intersect. President Harry S. Truman chose to recognize the modern State of Israel immediately upon its declaration of independence in 1948, and since then, America and Israel have bonded as allies committed to the values of life and liberty. With Israel constantly facing hostility and existential threats, the U.S. has generally stood alongside, even in often unfriendly diplomatic arenas like the UN. Moreover, while remaining committed to mitigating the decades-long Israeli-Palestinian conflict, our nation took a bold and powerfully symbolic step to reshape that debate during the Trump administration, by making the U.S. the first nation to open its embassy in Jerusalem.

God's Word very clearly tells us that those who bless Israel will be blessed, and that those who curse Israel will be cursed. We need not naively think that Israel is infallible. Israel does make mistakes, just as America does. But we are charged by God to stand faithfully with our ally. Quite simply, if we want God to bless America, then America must be a blessing to Israel.

PRAY

- ☐ Pray for the peace of Jerusalem and of all people of good will in Israel. May the peace of Christ overcome violence, belligerence, and hard hearts there.
- ☐ Pray that the U.S. will remain unwaveringly faithful to its ally. May leaders across the political spectrum seek blessing on our own land by being a blessing to Israel.
- ☐ Pray against efforts like the Boycott, Divestment, and Sanctions (BDS) movement, which demonizes not only Israel but also Jewish people in the U.S. and around the world. Antisemitism is evil, and it must be repelled.

ENGAGE

Phone your U.S. senators today and tell them that you stand firmly and unapologetically with Israel, and that you expect them to do the same.

Day 29: Generosity Abroad

The generous soul will be made rich, and he
who waters will also be watered himself.
(Proverbs 11:25)

Following the horrors of World War II, much of Europe lay in ruins. The Continent and its people were ravaged and susceptible to despair, a particularly dangerous situation with Stalin's communist regime threatening to fill the power vacuum left behind after Hitler's fall. U.S. Secretary of State George C. Marshall, who had helped win the war as Army chief of staff, had a plan.

In a 1947 speech at Harvard, Marshall called it "logical" for America to invest financially in the rebuilding of Europe. But even beyond fighting "hunger, poverty, desperation, and chaos," Marshall said, the purpose of this U.S. policy "should be the revival of a working economy in the world so as to permit the emergence of political and social conditions in which free institutions can exist."

Arguably, the Marshall Plan helped Western Europe on the path to recovery and helped contain the growing Soviet threat. And before long, the stark differences in the levels of freedom and prosperity on each side of the Iron Curtain became starkly evident. The "investment" thus seems to have been a good policy. It was surely a generous action. But perhaps there is more to consider here.

To be sure, one aspiration of many Americans has long been that we be a generous people. In fact, it is said that in the early 1800s, Frenchman Alexis de Tocqueville traveled around our young nation and was struck by instances of charity he witnessed. Consequently, many believe that de Tocqueville wound up observing that America's greatness is directly connected to America's goodness. It's an open question, though, whether de Tocqueville ever actually said that, as it's not actually found in his book *Democracy in America* or any of his other writings.

Still, even today Americans devote themselves to blessing others around the world in a spirit of generosity. We certainly give through our churches, missions organizations, and other ministries.

This country also gives through our government's foreign-aid programs. And though those programs reportedly make up only about 1% of our national budget, they send a powerful signal to our neighbors abroad that America values their lives, liberty, and pursuit of happiness.

But as with nonprofit giving, when it comes to U.S. government largesse, it's only wise to make sure that any forms of financial disbursement are handled honorably, efficiently, and responsibly. Indeed, the principles of justice demand no less, for the sake of the taxpayers.

Today, many observers are deeply concerned that the way our government dispenses foreign aid is too often wrong. Many are understandably questioning the money that's going to Iran, for example. In this case or any other, should our giving go to hostile, anti-America recipients? Wouldn't that money be better spent among needy nations without an ax to grind?

Then, too, there is our national debt. Is it God's will that, contrary to being a giver or lender nation, America should actually be a *debtor* nation, owing so much to other nations? That seems to be what we've come to.

At any rate, a commitment to generosity does not mean submitting to foolishness, frivolity, or fraud. This is especially true as concerns the hard-earned money of the American people.

But even as we strive to ensure proper safeguards and accountable stewardship, we should nonetheless continue to celebrate an underlying spirit of generosity. In fact, we must prayerfully keep up such a spirit. That pleases God. And by His grace, America can remain a compassionate and giving nation, if we will follow God and give according to wisdom.

PRAY

☐ Pray that Americans would remain a generous but also a wise people.

☐ Pray against waste and confused priorities in America's foreign-aid investments. May our public dollars be used effectively to meet such real needs as hunger, health, and shelter.

☐ Pray especially for Christian ministries that are active in relief work abroad. May any private or public investments directed to them strengthen their ability to meet physical needs even as they share the love of Christ boldly and beautifully.

ENGAGE

If you've never done so, contact a Christian relief organization and ask how you can be of practical help, and also how you can be praying for their work.

Day 30: International Religious Freedom

*You are my hiding place; You shall preserve me
from trouble; You shall surround me with songs of
deliverance. (Psalm 32:7)*

It is fitting as we approach the end of these 31 days of intercession for America that we return to where we began. We turn our minds again to America's first freedom: religious freedom.

Today we reflect on the great need to pray for religious liberty around the world. We face serious challenges in our homeland, to be sure, challenges we ignore at our own peril. However, as we turn our eyes outward, we find that 80% of the world's people live under significant restrictions on their religious freedoms. Observers have said that this foundational human right also happens to be among the most abused in the world. The cost of that abuse is very high. In fact, Sam Brownback, former U.S. Ambassador-at-Large for International Religious Freedom, has said: "If all nations had religious freedom, virtually all wars and conflicts would be eliminated."

Many who suffer the denial of their religious liberties worldwide are our brothers and sisters in Christ. Open Doors U.S., which works with churches to support Christian believers who are in harm's way, estimates that some 360 million Christians around the world are now suffering high levels of persecution and discrimination. Moreover, upwards of 2,000 churches and Christian buildings suffered attack in 2022, the organization says. Even more shockingly, more than 5,000 believers have been *murdered* for their faith in Jesus!

These dangers are high in some places that you might guess. North Korea, for example, is regularly at the top of the list of the most dangerous places for Christians. Middle East regimes, especially Iran, also rank high. But so do some places you might not expect, including the democratically governed nations of India and Nigeria, both of which can be brutally violent places for the followers of Christ.

Let's take a moment today to pray for our brothers and sisters who are suffering persecution. And let's pray also for people of other religious backgrounds who are facing danger. Ensuring religious liberty for all is foundational to nurturing security and freedom at home and abroad. And, as we explored earlier in this study, we know that it is as free creatures that God wants to meet us and welcome us into the fold of Him who is the way, the truth, and the life.

May God enable America to remain a beacon for religious freedom in a world threatened by darkness and oppression.

PRAY

☐ Pray that the current presidential administration will begin to prioritize international religious freedom in its foreign policy.

☐ Pray that our nation would press others, especially fellow democratic governments like India and Nigeria, to do all they can to thwart persecution of Christians and other religious minorities.

☐ Intercede for our 360 million brothers and sisters in Christ who face danger and discrimination around the world today.

ENGAGE

Is there any specific country or region of the world that God has put on your heart for prayer? Try to find a group of intercessors to join you in praying and fasting for the Christian believers suffering in that particular place. Pray that the light of Christ would dispel the darkness there. And if you need help with learning about specific needs or finding a group of intercessors to pray alongside, let us help you!

Day 31: Your Next Step

*Your word is a lamp to my feet and a light to my
path. (Psalm 119:105)*

Thank you for going through this 31-day challenge with us. Together we have explored and declared in detail many expressions of America's founding principles of life, liberty, and the pursuit of happiness.

Now we turn to *you*. What is on *your* heart today? What declaration is God calling you to make for our land? What next step does He desire for you as you pursue that conviction? He has given you a special heart and a voice uniquely empowered by His Spirit. Write below what God is telling you:

_____

_____

_____

PRAY

- ☐ Pray that God would reveal what specific declaration He has for you to make, and also that He would make known His direction to you.
- ☐ Ask the Lord to reveal a verse from Scripture that He wants you to press into for our nation.
- ☐ And pray that America would re-envision a path of life, liberty, and the true pursuit of happiness.

ENGAGE

IFA wants to support you as you intercede for our land. Contact our team through IFAPray.org or by calling 1-800-USA-PRAY and let us know that you've completed this study. We want to pray for you and with you (we'll do that immediately on the phone, if you like!), and we also want to send you a free resource to help you as you take your next step. Thank you again for your faithfulness!